GRAPHIC MYSTERIES
ATLANTIS
AND OTHER LOST CITIES

by Rob Shone

illustrated by Jim Eldridge

The Rosen Publishing Group, Inc., New York

Published in 2006 by The Rosen Publishing Group, Inc.
29 East 21st Street, New York, NY 10010

First edition, 2006

Designed and produced by
David West Books

Editor: Charlotte Cattermole, Kate Newport

Photo credits:
    Page 4, NASA; Page 5, Dan Brandenburg/iStockphoto.com; Page 45, Michael Owen/iStockphoto.com

Library of Congress Cataloging-in-Publication Data

Shone, Rob.
    Atlantis and other lost cities / by Rob Shone; illustrated by Jim Eldridge.
    p. cm. — (Graphic mysteries)
    Includes bibliographical references and index.
    ISBN 1-4042-0794-5 (lib. bdg.) — ISBN 1-4042-0809-7 (pbk.) — ISBN 1-4042-6262-8 (6 pack)
    1. Geographical myths. 2. Lost continents. I. Eldridge, Jim, ill.
    II. Title. III. Series.

GR940.S46 2005
398'.42—dc22

                                                2005017761

Manufactured in China

CONTENTS

HIDDEN PLACES

People have told stories of lost civilizations and their ancient cities for thousands of years. The mystery surrounding these lost cities still divides experts today. Did they exist at all? Where could they have been, and how did they vanish?

There are still many ancient sites waiting to be explored in Central America, such as this pre-Colombian ruin in Costa Rica.

ATLANTIS – It was the philosopher Plato who first described this beautiful but doomed city, in c. 400 B.C. Since then, historians and treasure seekers have tried to find out where Atlantis is and how it was destroyed. So far they have all failed.

EL DORADO – This is the legendary golden city that is thought to have been in South America. It is linked to stories of an ancient king, also named El Dorado (Spanish for "The Golden Man"), who covered himself in gold.

CAMELOT – Camelot is the legendary court of King Arthur. There are many theories about where in Great Britain it might have been, but there is still no hard evidence to prove that it existed at all.

Mu – A lost paradise known as Mu was once thought to have been the Garden of Eden. Experts believe that Mu was destroyed by a natural disaster, such as an earthquake or flooding. Some claim that the Pacific Islands are all that remain of Mu.

The Kingdom of Prester John – This legendary kingdom was ruled over by a Christian priest-king called Prester John. His kingdom was said to contain the fountain of life, and all John's subjects were happy, healthy, and peaceful. However, the legend also states that this paradise was almost impossible to reach.

Lyonesse – Connected to tales of King Arthur, Lyonesse was once a country beyond Lands' End in Cornwall, England. Legend says that a great storm blew up, and the sea covered the land. When Arthur returns, however, Lyonesse will again rise from the ocean waters.

Ogygia – Ogygia was the island of the goddess Calypso, a figure in Greek mytholgy. It was very cold and full of dark forests and scary beasts. Calpyso kept the hero Odysseus here for many years as a sort of willing prisoner.

This Inca city was discovered at the top of Machu Picchu at the beginning of the twentieth century. Nobody knows what happened to the people who once lived there.

LOST CITIES

Explorers and scientists have searched all over the world to find anything that could lead to the discovery of these legendary lost cities. Historical writings, myths and folk tales, and artifacts all leave clues to where such places may be found.

A City Beneath the Sea
Plato first told the story of how Atlantis was destroyed. He described it as being located on a large island in the ocean west of the Pillars of Hercules. Since then, evidence of past civilizations that may have been Atlantis, such as human bones and tools, have been found in places around the world, including, near Thera, Greece, and off the west coast of Cuba.

GREECE

Thera

① CRETE

MEDITERRANEAN SEA

FLORIDA

BAHAMAS

②

Bimini Islands

CUBA

④

①

②

③

A world map showing the locations of the smaller maps.

TREASURE HUNT

In 1542, a party of conquistadors, led by the Spaniard Gonzalo Pizzaro, set out on an expedition deep into the heart of the Amazon. They were searching for El Dorado, the city of gold that Indians said lay hidden in the jungle. When Orellana finally returned to Spain, he brought with him magical tales of a lost civilization packed with riches. For 500 years, explorers have continued to search for El Dorado.

Inca gold cup

MEDIEVAL MYSTERY

The legend of King Arthur and his medieval court at Camelot is known throughout the world. It tells of how a powerful and holy king, along with his chivalrous Knights of the Round Table, united his people and defeated evil. However, nobody really knows whether a ruler called Arthur or Camelot actually existed. Even so, many places still claim to have been the site of Camelot.

This map of Great Britain shows some of the places where Camelot might have been.

ATLANTIS

SEPTEMBER 1968. LOCAL FISHING GUIDE, "BONEFISH" SAM ELLIS, DROPPED HIS ANCHOR. HIS FLAT-BOTTOMED SKIFF FLOATED IN THE SHALLOWS OFF THE WEST COAST OF BIMINI, AN ISLAND IN THE BAHAMAS...

HE WAS MORE USED TO TAKING TOURISTS OUT ON FISHING TRIPS. TODAY HIS PASSENGER WAS INTERESTED IN SOMETHING OTHER THAN FISHING.

LET ME GET THIS RIGHT, DOC — I'VE BROUGHT YOU ALL THE WAY OUT HERE JUST SO YOU CAN LOOK AT SOME **OLD STONES**?

...IF WHAT PEOPLE HAVE TOLD ME ABOUT THEM IS TRUE, THOSE OLD STONES MIGHT BE VALUABLE.

I'M AN ARCHAEOLOGIST, BONEFISH. IT'S MY JOB TO LOOK AT OLD STONES. BESIDES...

I'LL SEE YOU IN ABOUT TWENTY MINUTES.

BLOOOSH!!

DR. MASON VALENTINE DISAPPEARED...

...BENEATH THE DARK BLUE WATERS.

BACK ON THE SKIFF...

I'VE NEVER SEEN ANYTHING LIKE IT, BONEFISH! **HUGE** BLOCKS OF STONE – **HUNDREDS** OF THEM – NEATLY LAID OUT ON THE SEABED.

IT LOOKED LIKE AN **UNDERWATER ROAD!** I FOLLOWED IT AS FAR AS I COULD UNTIL MY AIR GOT LOW.

BELIEVE ME, I KNOW STONES, AND THAT ROAD WASN'T FORMED NATURALLY. IT WAS MADE BY PEOPLE!

WHO PUT IT THERE, DOC?

HAVE YOU HEARD OF SOMEONE CALLED PLATO?

UM...NO.

PLATO WAS AN ANCIENT GREEK PHILOSOPHER. HE ONCE TOLD THE STORY OF A MIGHTY CITY THAT WAS DESTROYED THOUSANDS OF YEARS BEFORE HE WAS BORN.

THIS CITY RULED OVER A HUGE ISLAND, WEST OF THE PILLARS OF HERCULES.

THE PILLARS OF HERCULES?

IT'S WHAT THEY CALLED THE STRAITS OF GIBRALTAR THEN.

SO?

WE'RE WEST OF GIBRALTAR. MAYBE THIS ROAD IS PART OF PLATO'S LOST CITY.

DID PLATO HAVE A NAME FOR THIS CITY?

YES, BONEFISH. HE CALLED IT – ATLANTIS!

ATLANTIS – ISLAND HOME OF POSEIDON, THE GOD OF THE SEA. POSEIDON FELL IN LOVE WITH CLEITO, A HUMAN, AND BUILT THE CITY OF ATLANTIS FOR HER.

ON A HILL AT THE CENTER OF THE CITY STOOD THE TEMPLE OF POSEIDON.

HERE, THE TEN SONS OF CLEITO WORSHIPPED THEIR FATHER AND RULED WISELY OVER THE ISLAND.

THE CENTER OF THE CITY WAS CIRCLED BY THREE CANALS AND BY THREE GREAT WALLS. A FOURTH CANAL LINKED THEM ALL TO THE SEA.

TEMPLE OF POSEIDON

INNER CANAL

OUTER CANAL

CANAL TO SEA

OUTSIDE THE THIRD WALL...

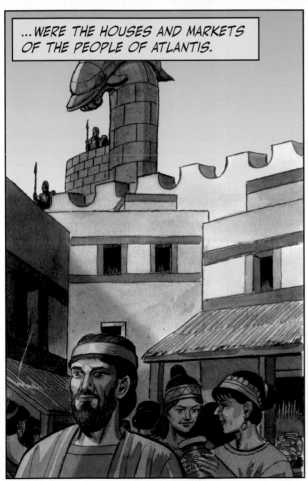

...WERE THE HOUSES AND MARKETS OF THE PEOPLE OF ATLANTIS.

BEYOND THE CITY LAY A FERTILE PLAIN THAT STRETCHED TO THE DISTANT MOUNTAINS.

NO MATTER WHAT TIME OF YEAR, THERE WAS ALWAYS ENOUGH FOOD FOR EVERYONE. FROM THE VERY SMALL...

...TO THE VERY LARGE.

THE ROCKS OF ATLANTIS WERE RICH IN PRECIOUS METALS AND GEMS. THE ATLANTEANS BECAME WEALTHY BY TRADING WITH THEIR NEIGHBORS.

MEANWHILE, ZEUS, LORD OF THE GODS, SAW HOW EVIL AND CORRUPT THE PEOPLE OF ATLANTIS HAD BECOME. HE DECIDED THAT THEY MUST BE **PUNISHED.**

IN ONE TERRIBLE DAY AND NIGHT, THE GODS CAUSED THE WATERS AROUND ATLANTIS TO RISE. BOTH CITY AND ISLAND WERE SWALLOWED BY THE FURIOUS WAVES OF THE SEA.

WHEN MORNING CAME, ATLANTIS HAD VANISHED.

SO, AFTER BEING LOST UNDER THE WAVES FOR NEARLY 12,000 YEARS, HAD DR. VALENTINE AND BONEFISH SAM FINALLY FOUND ATLANTIS IN THE CARIBBEAN? SOME PEOPLE PLACE ATLANTIS MUCH CLOSER TO GREECE – ON THE ISLAND OF THERA, (NOW CALLED SANTORINI), IN THE MEDITERRANEAN SEA.

LONG BEFORE PLATO'S TIME, A MIGHTY CIVILIZATION GREW ON THE ISLAND OF CRETE IN THE MEDITERRANEAN– THE MINOANS. THEIR SEA POWER HAD MADE THE MINOANS WEALTHY, AND THEIR CITIES AND PALACES WERE THE MARVEL OF THEIR AGE.

THERA, WITH ITS FERTILE SOIL, WAS A LIVELY MINOAN COLONY. ON ITS STEEP-SIDED SLOPES WERE MINOAN SETTLEMENTS, VILLAGES, AND A ROYAL PALACE.

AT THE ISLAND'S HEART, THOUGH, WAS A VOLCANO. IT HAD BEEN QUIET FOR MANY YEARS–BUT IT WAS ABOUT TO **AWAKEN AGAIN!**

BRUMMBLE!!

KRUNCKRR!

KARABOOMMM!!!

IN AROUND 400 B.C.,
THE VOLCANO EXPLODED,
RIPPING THE ISLAND APART.

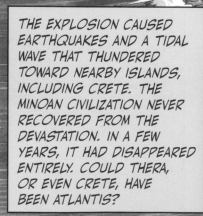

THE EXPLOSION CAUSED
EARTHQUAKES AND A TIDAL
WAVE THAT THUNDERED
TOWARD NEARBY ISLANDS,
INCLUDING CRETE. THE
MINOAN CIVILIZATION NEVER
RECOVERED FROM THE
DEVASTATION. IN A FEW
YEARS, IT HAD DISAPPEARED
ENTIRELY. COULD THERA,
OR EVEN CRETE, HAVE
BEEN ATLANTIS?

MANY SCHOLARS HAVE CLAIMED TO KNOW WHERE ATLANTIS IS, PLACING IT ALL OVER FROM THE JUNGLES OF SOUTH AMERICA...

...TO THE ICY WASTELANDS OF THE ANTARCTIC.

PERHAPS ATLANTIS WAS NEVER MORE THAN A LEGEND.

YET PEOPLE STILL HOPE THAT ITS RUINS LIE HIDDEN SOMEWHERE, JUST WAITING TO BE FOUND...

THE END

EL DORADO

IN APRIL 1925, COLONEL PERCY HARRISON FAWCETT LEFT CUIBÁ, IN BRAZIL, AND WALKED INTO THE DENSE MATTO GROSSO JUNGLE OF SOUTH AMERICA.

WITH HIM WERE HIS YOUNG SON, JACK, AND JACK'S FRIEND, RALEIGH RIMELL.

FAWCETT HAD HEARD MANY STRANGE TALES OVER THE YEARS OF ANCIENT RUINS, CRUMBLING IN THE DARK HEART OF THE JUNGLE.

BUT ONE STORY SEEMED DIFFERENT. IT TOLD OF A SECRET CITY, FULL OF RICHES AND WEALTH, A CITY OF MYSTERY – AND FAWCETT BELIEVED HE KNEW WHERE IT WAS. HE CALLED IT CITY "Z."

WHAT WAS CITY "Z"? COULD FAWCETT AND HIS PARTY HAVE BEEN SEARCHING FOR THE LOST CITY OF EL DORADO?

FAWCETT THOUGHT THEY WOULD BE GONE FOR FEWER THAN TWO YEARS. HE WAS MISTAKEN. THEY WERE NEVER SEEN AGAIN.

NO ONE KNOWS WHAT HAPPENED TO FAWCETT, HIS SON, OR RALEIGH RIMELL. HAD THE LEGEND OF EL DORADO CLAIMED THREE MORE LIVES?

WHERE DID THE LEGEND OF EL DORADO BEGIN? IN 1531, THE SPANIARD, FRANCISCO PIZARRO, LEADING 177 MEN, LANDED ON THE WESTERN COAST OF SOUTH AMERICA. IN JUST A FEW MONTHS THIS SMALL BAND OF SOLDIERS CONQUERED THE MIGHTY INCA EMPIRE.

THE INCA HAD NO ANSWER TO SPANISH GUNS AND CANNONS.

THE INCA KING, ATAHUALPA, WAS CAPTURED AND HELD FOR RANSOM BY PIZARRO. THE SPANIARDS SET THE PRICE FOR HIS RELEASE...

HAVE YOU EVER SEEN SO MUCH GOLD IN ONE PLACE BEFORE?! **A WHOLE ROOM** FILLED FROM FLOOR TO CEILING WITH IT!

AND THERE ARE TWO MORE FILLED WITH SILVER! IT'S NOT ENOUGH TO SAVE THEIR KING FROM THE EXECUTIONER, THOUGH.

WHERE DO YOU THINK IT ALL CAME FROM?

I DON'T KNOW, BUT I BET YOU THERE'S MORE TREASURE OUT THERE.

THE INCA ARE CLEVER. I THINK THIS IS JUST A FRACTION OF THEIR GOLD. THEY'VE HIDDEN THE REST IN THE MOUNTAINS OR IN THE JUNGLE.

SOON, RUMORS SPREAD THROUGHOUT THE SPANISH CAMP...

THE INCA CALL IT MANOA, AN ENTIRE CITY OF GOLD, RULED BY A GOLDEN KING.

THE WALLS OF THE BUILDINGS ARE MADE OF SOLID GOLD, AND THE STREETS ARE PAVED WITH INGOTS OF PURE SILVER.

EVEN EVERYDAY THINGS – SPOONS, PLATES, CUPS – ARE ALL MADE OF GOLD.

SO WHERE IS THIS CITY OF GOLD?

I DON'T KNOW, BUT THE INCA DO, AND THEY CAN BE **MADE** TO TELL US EXACTLY WHERE IT IS!

THE SPANISH LUSTED AFTER THIS TREASURE. THEY CALLED THE GOLDEN CITY EL DORADO, AND THEY MEANT TO FIND IT!

BY 1539, THE SPANISH HAD BROUGHT THE WHOLE INCA EMPIRE UNDER THEIR CONTROL. AT QUITO, A TOWN TO THE NORTH OF SPAIN'S NEW TERRITORY, 1541...

WHAT'S HAPPENING DOWN THERE?

IT'S THE NEW GOVERNOR. HE AND SOME OF HIS MEN ARE GOING OFF TO FIND OUT WHAT'S ON THE OTHER SIDE OF THE MOUNTAINS TO THE EAST.

THE NEW GOVERNOR OF QUITO WAS GONZALO, YOUNGER BROTHER OF FRANCISCO PIZARRO.

HE CHOSE HIS FRIEND AND COUSIN, FRANCISCO DE ORELLANA, AS HIS SECOND IN COMMAND. THEIR MISSION WAS TO FIND EL DORADO.

IN FEBRUARY 1541, THE LARGE EXPEDITION LEFT QUITO FOR THE FOOTHILLS OF THE ANDES.

THEY MADE GOOD PROGRESS AT FIRST...

WHAT ARE YOUR PLANS, GONZALO?

THE NATIVES SPEAK OF A SACRED WATERFALL NEARBY. ATAHUALPA'S GOLD IS THERE! I AM SURE OF IT.

THEY FOUND THE WATERFALL...

SO, THE TREASURE'S NOT HERE AFTER ALL.

NO. THE WATERFALL GUARDS ATAHUALPA'S SPIRIT, NOT HIS GOLD. LET'S MOVE ON.

IN THE MOUNTAINS, THEIR JOURNEY BECAME HARDER.

SIX MONTHS LATER, EAST OF THE MOUNTAINS...

NOTHING! JUST ENDLESS SCRUB AND JUNGLE AS FAR AS YOU CAN SEE.

WELL, EL DORADO'S NOT HERE EITHER!

THEY HAD BIGGER WORRIES, HOWEVER. THEIR FOOD WAS RUNNING OUT.

THE NATIVE GUIDES ARE DYING, SOON IT WILL BE OUR TURN.

GONZALO! WE MUST TURN BACK! THERE IS NO FOOD HERE. THIS IS JUST A BARREN WASTELAND.

I WILL NOT BE DEFEATED, FRANCISCO! ORDER THE MEN TO BUTCHER THE HORSES. WE WILL EAT THEM UNTIL WE FIND FOOD, FARTHER ON.

THE SPANIARDS BUILT A RAFT TO CARRY THE SICK AND THEIR SUPPLIES. THE EXPEDITION SLOWLY MADE ITS WAY DOWN THE COCA RIVER.

AFTER A MONTH, GONZALO DECIDED TO STOP. THERE WERE FEW NATIVES LEFT ALIVE NOW, AND THE SPANIARDS HAD STARTED TO DIE AS WELL. THE MEN WERE CLOSE TO MUTINY.

FRANCISCO, I WANT YOU TO TAKE THE BOAT AND THE STRONGEST MEN LEFT. TRAVEL DOWN THE RIVER AND FIND FOOD. YOU'RE OUR LAST HOPE FOR SURVIVAL.

ON CHRISTMAS DAY, 1541, FRANCISO AND FIFTY-SEVEN MEN, LEFT PIZARRO AND DRIFTED DOWN THE COCA RIVER.

I'LL BE BACK IN TWO WEEKS.

FROM THE COCA RIVER, FRANCISCO ENTERED THE BIGGER NAPO RIVER...

THE CURRENT IS TOO FAST AND STRONG! WE'LL NEVER BE ABLE TO GET BACK TO GONZALO. WE HAVE NO CHOICE BUT TO GO DOWNRIVER.

AFTER MANY DAYS, THE RIVER WIDENED AND THE CURRENT SLOWED. FRANCISCO'S MEN WERE STARVING, BUT THEY HAD REACHED THE AMAZON RAIN FOREST – AND FOOD!

LOOK!

QUICK! SHOOT IT, SOMEONE!

MEANWHILE, BACK ON THE COCA RIVER, GONZALO WAS WAITING. HIS FOOD WAS ALMOST GONE, ALONG WITH HIS DREAM OF FINDING EL DORADO.

COMMANDER, IT'S BEEN MORE THAN TWO WEEKS NOW. FRANCISCO DE ORELLANA IS NOT COMING BACK. WHAT SHALL WE DO?

COMMANDER?

FRANCISCO, YOU WERE MY FRIEND! WHY HAVE YOU DESERTED ME? I SHALL HAVE MY REVENGE!

WE WILL GO BACK TO QUITO.

A FEW HUNDRED MILES TO THE EAST, FRANCISCO LIKE GONZALO, HAD ABANDONED HOPE OF FINDING THE GOLDEN CITY.

HIS BOAT DRIFTED SLOWLY DOWN THE NAPO RIVER...

...UNTIL IT REACHED THE MIGHTY AMAZON RIVER.

LAKE GUATAVITA, NEAR BOGOTA, IN COLOMBIA.

THE SPANISH LEARNED THAT EACH YEAR, THE KING OF THE LOCAL CHIBCHA PEOPLE, COVERED FROM HEAD TO TOE IN GOLD DUST, WAS ROWED OUT TO THE MIDDLE OF THE LAKE.

GOLD OFFERINGS WERE MADE BY THE KING AND THE WATCHING CROWDS.

FINALLY, THE KING WASHED OFF THE GOLD DUST.

IN 1580, DON ANTONIO SEPULVEDA FOUND LAKE GUATAVITA.

THINK OF ALL THE GOLD THAT MUST LIE AT THE LAKE'S BOTTOM!

SEPULVEDA HAD A PLAN...

THE LAKE SITS IN A NATURAL HOLLOW ABOVE THE VALLEY.

IF WE CUT A CHANNEL THERE, THE LAKE WILL DRAIN AND REVEAL ITS RICHES!

THE SPANIARD USED THOUSANDS OF LOCAL NATIVES AS SLAVES. THEY STARTED TO CUT A NOTCH IN THE LAKE'S RIM TO LET OUT THE WATER.

THE LEVEL OF THE LAKE STARTED TO DROP. BUT THEN...

THE CHANNEL WALLS ARE STARTING TO COLLAPSE! RUN!

WE HAVE DISTURBED THE GODS. THEY ARE ANGRY WITH US!

COME BACK! I ORDER YOU TO COME BACK!

SEPULVEDA WAS FORCED TO GIVE UP.

THE LAKE WAS LEFT IN PEACE FOR OVER 400 YEARS UNTIL, IN 1912...

BOOOM!!

GENTLEMEN, WE'RE BRINGING MODERN TECHNOLOGY TO TREASURE HUNTING! WITH OUR MODERN MINING GEAR, WE CAN BLAST A TUNNEL INTO THE HILLSIDE, EMPTY THE LAKE – AND HELP OURSELVES TO THE GOLD!

THE WATERS OF THE LAKE DRAINED AWAY...

...AND IN ITS PLACE...

MUD! ALL THE GOLD SANK INTO IT, AND NOW THE SUN HAS BAKED IT DRY. IT'S AS HARD AS CONCRETE! IT'LL TAKE YEARS TO DIG IT OUT!

KTCHNCKK!

LIKE SEPULVEDA, THE MINERS GAVE UP THEIR SEARCH. OVER THE NEXT SIXTY YEARS, OTHERS TRIED AND FAILED TO FIND THE GOLD, AND TO THIS DAY, NOBODY KNOWS FOR SURE WHERE EL DORADO EXISTS.

THE END

CAMELOT

A FIFTH-CENTURY A.D. BRITISH MONASTERY...

??!

THE ROMAN LEGIONS THAT HAD OCCUPIED THE ISLANDS OF BRITAIN FOR SO LONG HAD FINALLY GONE. BUT THEY HAD LEFT THE COUNTRY DEFENSELESS. GERMANIC TRIBES FROM THE EUROPEAN MAINLAND SAW THEIR CHANCE.

ANGLES, SAXONS, AND JUTES MOVED WEST, DESTROYING THE MONASTERIES AND THE KNOWLEDGE AND LEARNING THEY POSSESSED. HISTORIES WERE LOST, AND THE PRESENT WENT UNRECORDED. BECAUSE OF THE DESTRUCTION OF BOOKS AND MANUSCRIPTS CONTAINING SO MUCH KNOWLEDGE...

FLWHOOOSH!

...THIS ERA BECAME KNOWN AS THE DARK AGES.

THE INVADERS MOVED FROM PLACE TO PLACE, BURNING CHURCHES AND MONASTERIES WHEREVER THEY FOUND THEM. BUT THEN, STRANGELY, THEIR MARCH WEST SLOWED, AND FINALLY STOPPED.

LEGENDS SAY THAT ONE MAN WAS RESPONSIBLE FOR TURNING BACK THE ANGLO-SAXON INVASION. A GREAT KING UNITED THE PEOPLE AND STOOD AGAINST THE FOREIGN ENEMY, WINNING BATTLE AFTER BATTLE.

HE WAS ARTHUR, KING OF THE BRITONS. THE FINAL VICTORY CAME AT MOUNT BADON. THERE, MORE THAN 900 WESTERN SAXONS FELL BENEATH ARTHUR'S ENCHANTED SWORD, EXCALIBUR.

EVERY KING NEEDS A CASTLE–AND ARTHUR'S WAS CALLED CAMELOT.

FROM CAMELOT, THE KING AND HIS QUEEN, GUINEVERE, RULED THE LAND.

TO HELP HIM GOVERN AND DEFEND THE KINGDOM, ARTHUR FORMED A COUNCIL OF KNIGHTS–THE KNIGHTS OF THE ROUND TABLE.

FOR ADVICE, ARTHUR WOULD TURN TO MERLIN, THE MAGICIAN.

FOR MANY YEARS ARTHUR RULED THE LAND WISELY. HIS KNIGHTS SPENT THEIR TIME JOUSTING...

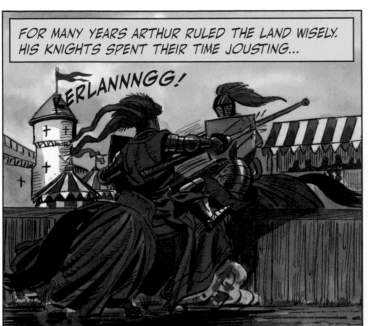

KERLANNNGG!

...OR RIDING OUT TO HELP THE PEOPLE IN TIMES OF TROUBLE.

BUT ARTHUR HAD ENEMIES AT COURT. HIS NEPHEW, MORDRED, WAS JEALOUS OF ARTHUR'S POWER AND POPULARITY. MORDRED TURNED THE KNIGHTS AGAINST EACH OTHER, AND SOON THERE WAS CIVIL WAR.

THE CIVIL WAR ENDED AT THE RIVER CAMLANN. THERE, ARTHUR FOUGHT HIS FINAL BATTLE. AS MOST OF THE KNIGHTS FROM BOTH SIDES LAY DEAD AND DYING, ARTHUR KILLED MORDRED. BUT IN DOING SO, HE HIMSELF WAS FATALLY WOUNDED.

WITH ARTHUR GONE, CAMELOT SOON BECAME A FAINT MEMORY, MORE LEGEND THAN HISTORY.

HAD LESLEY ALCOCK FOUND CAMELOT?

IT'S FROM THE RIGHT PERIOD, AND IT'S LARGE ENOUGH TO HAVE BEEN AN IMPORTANT DEFENSIVE STRONGHOLD.

IT WOULDN'T HAVE LOOKED LIKE THE CAMELOT OF LEGEND, THOUGH.

CADBURY CASTLE, C.490 A.D.

THE CELTIC TRIBES OF THE SOUTHWEST HAD ALWAYS BEEN MIGHTY. EVEN THE ROMANS FOUND THEM HARD TO CONTROL. WHEN THE ROMANS LEFT, IT WAS AT CADBURY CASTLE THAT THESE CELTIC BRITONS MADE A STAND AGAINST THE GERMANIC INVADERS.

A NEARBY VILLAGE...

...WAS BEING WATCHED.

A SAXON RAID!

THE SURVIVORS FLED...

...TO THE ONLY PLACE WHERE THEY KNEW THEY WOULD BE SAFE...

...THE HILL FORT AT CADBURY.

INSIDE THE FORT WERE KITCHENS, WORKSHOPS, AND HOMES FOR THE SOLDIERS AND LOCAL PEOPLE.

BUT WHO WAS THE FORT'S LORD? WHICH CHIEFTAIN WAS STONG ENOUGH TO KEEP THE VARIOUS LOCAL TRIBES AND KIN GROUPS FROM FIGHTING EACH OTHER?

AT THE FORT'S CENTER WAS THE GREAT HALL, AND INSIDE...

...SAT THE FORT'S CHIEFTAIN.

AFTER LISTENING TO THE VILLAGERS' STORY...

...THE CHIEFTAIN AND HIS TRIBAL CHIEFS AND CAPTAINS PLANNED THEIR COUNTERATTACK ON THE RAIDERS.

THE CHIEFTAIN AND HIS WARRIORS WERE READY...

...THEY TRACKED DOWN THE ENEMY...

...AND ATTACKED!

MANY PLACES IN BRITAIN HAVE CLAIMED TO BE ARTHUR'S CAMELOT. BUT THERE CAN BE ONLY ONE.

THE WHEREABOUTS OF THE TRUE CAMELOT IS STILL HIDDEN BY THE PASSING OF TIME.

THE END

FACT OR FICTION?

Before the existence of any of these lost civilizations can be proven, conclusive archaeological evidence must be found. Although research is being carried out at sites across the world, so far most evidence we have comes from folk tales and unreliable written sources.

GRAPHIC MYSTERIES
LOST CITIES

STONES ON THE SEAFLOOR

Maybe Plato did not mean Atlantis to be taken literally, but as a metaphor. Philosophers often used dialogue to express their ideas through argument, and Plato's account was written as a conversation between characters. Why, then, have people taken his story of a lost continent, with its improbable set of alternating rings of sea and land, as truth? Perhaps it is our knowledge of real disasters, such as the volcanic eruption that destroyed Pompeii, that makes us realize that places can just disappear.

Underwater exploration of both ancient and modern sites has become an important part of archaeology.

GOLD IN THE JUNGLE

The most interesting part of the El Dorado legend is that it is a European invention. A few years after Orellana's expedition, the Spanish returned to the Amazon in search of the kingdoms he described. They found nothing. Was Orellana lying to impress the Spanish court and find fame, like the other explorers who had found other civilizations in South America? Did his story become so famous just because it captured the imagination of a Europe determined to find and exploit the wealth of the new world?

Could a South American king, like the one above, have held the key to El Dorado's secrets?

Could Camelot have looked like this? Harlech Castle in Wales (above) was built not long after the French poet, Chrétien de Troyes, first mentioned Camelot by name in the twelfth century.

THE AGE OF CHIVALRY?

If there was a real King Arthur, he would not have been the romantic hero we think of today. There was no medieval king named Arthur. He was more likely to have been a Celtic warlord living in the Dark Ages, and he would not have lived in a grand palace, like the Camelot of legend. However, there is evidence at places like Cadbury, that an important leader like Arthur did once exist.

GLOSSARY

Angles Germanic people from Denmark who invaded Great Britain in the fifth and sixth centuries A.D.

archaeology The study of historical remains, such as relics.

barren A place that is bleak and or does not produce many crops.

Britons Native people in Great Britain, at the time of the Romans.

chieftain A leader of a tribe or tribes.

chivalry Medieval knightly system that valued the honoring and serving of women and defending those in need of protection.

civil war A war between different groups from the same country.

civilization A culture that has reached an advanced stage in social development.

colony Group of people originally from one country now occupying or ruling another territory on behalf of the mother country.

conclusive Evidence that is so strong that it puts an end to debate.

conquistadors Spanish conquerors of South America.

Dark Ages Period in European history, c. A.D. 500 until A.D.1000, in which civilization was said to be in decline.

enchanted To be influenced, controlled or dazzled by someone or something.

expedition A journey undertaken for a specific purpose.

exploit To unfairly make use of something or someone.

Inca The Quechuan people of Peru.

ingot An amount of metal molded into a convenient shape.

Jutes Germanic people who invaded England and settled in Kent.

knight A soldier of noble birth who served his king.

manuscripts Ancient documents written by hand.

marvel To be surprised at something, often because of its beauty.

medieval Historical period in Europe from 1000 to A.D. 1500.

monastery An enclosed community where monks live and work.

mortal Subject to eventual death. Humans are mortal.

philosopher A person who seeks wisdom or knowledge. The word philosophy means "love of knowledge."

plain A large area of country that has no trees.

Pompeii A city in southwest Italy that was destroyed by an eruption of the volcano Vesuvius in A.D. 79.

Roman legion The principal unit of the Roman army containing 5,000 men.

Saxons Germanic tribe that conquered England in the ninth century.

skiff A small, flat-bottomed rowing boat.

Victorians People who lived during the reign of Britain's Queen Victoria (1837–1901).

FOR MORE INFORMATION

ORGANIZATIONS

Smithsonian National Museum of Natural History
10th Street and Constitution Avenue, NW
Washington, DC 20560
Web site: http://www.mnh.si.edu/

University of Pennsylvania Museum of Archaeology and
Anthropology
3260 South Street
Philadelphia, PA 19104
(215) 898-4000
Web site: http://www.museum.upenn.edu/

FOR FURTHER READING

Bellingham, David. *The Kingfisher Book of Mythology: Gods,
Goddesses, and Heroes from Around the World.* London, England:
Kingfisher Publications, Plc., 2001.

Donkin, Andrew. *Atlantis: The Lost City?* New York: DK Publishing,
2000.

Foss, Michael. *The World of Camelot: King Arthur and the Knights
of the Round Table.* New York: Sterling Publishing Company, Inc.,
1998.

Hemming, John. *The Search for El Dorado.* London, England:
Phoenix Press, 2001.

Rosenberg, Aaron. *Atlantis (Unsolved Mysteries).* New York: The
Rosen Publishing Group, Inc., 2002.

INDEX

Web Sites

Due to the changing nature of Internet links, the Rosen Publishing Group, Inc., has developed an online list of Web sites related to the subject of this book. This site is updated regularly. Please use this link to access the list:
http://www.rosenlinks.com/grmy/aolc